Old Collieston and Slains

Ellie Ingram

The Slains coast was ideal for the landing and concealment of contraband and at the beginning of the nineteenth century excisemen from the Preventive Station kept their schooner anchored in the bay at Perthudden (Port Thuddan), north of the distinctive rock pillar called Puirman, which can be seen in the upper left of this photograph. Fishing and farming communities rarely socialised, but in Slains they did join together in smuggling to avoid paying taxes to the detested House of Hanover. Fishermen would bring the goods ashore and farmers would be waiting to transport the contraband by horse and cart to secret hiding places in local farms and cottar houses. Rumours have persisted over the years that secret passages still exist under some farm kitchens, leading to nearby caves where smuggled goods would have been temporarily stored prior to concealment. Goods were also hidden temporarily in secret caches on the links of Forvie. These caches would have been at least ten feet deep, beyond the depth of penetration of an exciseman's six-feet probe.

ISBN 9781840335958

**The publishers regret that they cannot supply
copies of any pictures featured in this book.**

Acknowledgements

The author wishes to thank the following for their assistance during her research: Charles Esson, Ken Ingram, Jack Page, Rear Admiral Steve Ritchie and the staff of the Local Studies Department of Aberdeenshire Libraries Headquarters, Oldmeldrum.

Further Reading

The books listed below were used by the author during her research. None of them is available from Stenlake Publishing. Those interested in finding out more are advised to contact their local bookshop or reference library.

The Road to Collieston Pier – A Celebration of the Pier's Centenary (1994)
The Statistical Account of Scotland (1793)
The New Statistical Account of Scotland (1843)
Margaret Aitken, *Six Buchan Villages Re-visited* (2004)
Peter F. Anson, *Fishing Boats and Fisher Folk on the East Coast of Scotland* (1930)
Ian Carter, *Farm Life in Northeast Scotland 1840–1914* (1979)
Victoria E. Clark, *The Port of Aberdeen* (1921)
Francis H. Groome, *Ordnance Gazetteer of Scotland* (1885)
Rev J.B. Pratt, *Buchan* (4th edition of 1858 original, 1901)
David W. Summers, *Fishing off the Knuckle – the Fishing Villages of Buchan* (1988)
Fenton Wyness, *Spots from the Leopard* (1971)

Introduction

The parish of Slains on the north-east Aberdeenshire coast is triangular in shape, approximately seven miles long and five miles across at its widest point, and covers an area of some 9,276 acres. It is bounded on the east by the North Sea and on the south-west by the River Ythan. The parishes of Cruden and Logie Buchan lie to the north and west respectively and the Forvie Burn flows south-west along the western border to the Ythan. The parish of Forvie, incorporated in the parish of Slains in 1573, is situated between Collieston and the River Ythan and was declared a National Nature Reserve in 1959.

The word Slains is said to signify 'health' in the Gaelic language. The origin of Collieston cannot be verified but in Robertson's Index (1408) it was referred to as 'Collystoun' and in the 1707 parish register it was called Seatown of Colleston. Evidence that people have been in the area for thousands of years has been found on the links of Forvie where excavations have unearthed flints, shell middens, discarded animal bones and kerb cairns.

Among the sand dunes stand the ruins of the twelfth-century Forvie Kirk, all that remains of a settlement buried by sand during a nine-day storm in the fifteenth century. Legend has it that the storm was the result of a curse placed upon the village by the laird of Forvie's three daughters, who had been dispossessed of their heritage and taken by ship from Scotland to France: 'If ever maydenis malysone / Dyd licht upon dry land / Lat nocht bee fund in Furvye's glebys / Bot thystl, bente and sande.'

In 1696, 36 fishermen lived in 'Collestowne', at that time the largest fishing community north of the River Tay. In 1840 Collieston had 89 houses and a population of 167. By 1871 the population had risen to 442 and in Old Castle there were fourteen houses and a population of 80.

King Robert the Bruce gifted the lands of Slains to Sir Gilbert Hay in the fourteenth century in recognition of his loyalty during the Wars of Independence. For centuries the majority of land and property in the parish, the Slains Estate, was owned by the Hay family, the Earls of Erroll. The estate was sold in 1791 to Sir Alexander Callander of Crighton MP and, after Sir Alexander's death the following year, the estate was bought by Colonel John Gordon of Cluny.

In the late nineteenth century the two principal heritors in Slains were Lady Gordon Cathcart of Cluny, widow of Colonel John Gordon, and Mr John Gordon Cumming of Pitlurg, owner of the land and property at Leask. The House of Leask, originally a Cumming property in the early eighteenth century, was renamed Gordon Lodge after the marriage of Barbara Cumming to Dr Alexander Gordon of Hilton and Straloch. Their grandson renamed it Pitlurg after the family's ancestral lands in Banffshire. In 1826/27 his son, Captain Gordon Cumming Skene of Pitlurg, Dyce and Parkhill, commissioned Aberdeen architect Archibald Simpson to build the House of Leask, returning the property to its original name. The house burnt down in 1927 but was rebuilt in the late twentieth century. Situated on the farm of Knapsleask are the ruins of a chapel, believed to have been built in the fifteenth century and dedicated to St Adamnan.

For centuries most of the population of Slains earned their living by fishing or farming, but a few individuals were also involved in other types of work. In 1791, when the population was recorded as 1,117, there were 146 fishermen, 60 farmers, one clergyman, five merchants, one schoolmaster, seven ale-sellers, five smiths, two carpenters, five square-wrights, seven weavers, ten shoemakers, fourteen tailors and six millers. The 24 people classed as 'poor' would have received an annual sum of money from the Parochial Fund, money raised from the church's weekly collection.

The Education (Scotland) Act of 1872 led to the setting up of parish school boards and Slains School Board held their first meeting on 21 April 1873. Of the 269 school age children in the parish, 98 were enrolled at the Parish School, 31 at the Bruce Hay Girls' School, 21 at the Free Church School, seven at Elspet Kennedy's School, while 23 went to schools outwith the parish and 89 children were not enrolled at any school.

On 2 August 1897 an intermediate railway station was opened at Pitlurg and trains on the Ellon–Peterhead branch line of the Great North of Scotland Railway stopped there. There was talk of a branch line coming into Collieston, but this never happened. Pitlurg Station closed to regular passenger traffic on 31 October 1933.

Collieston's fishermen were dealt a blow when, as many had predicted, sand from Aberdeen Bay began to accumulate in the harbour after the construction of the pier in 1894. The silting up of the harbour, combined with the advent of steam trawling, resulted in many young fishermen leaving the village to pursue their trade in Torry and Peterhead. Consequently, there was a sharp decline in the number of children attending school and by 1900 the roll had fallen by 30%, from 80 to 56.

Throughout the latter half of the twentieth century the farming community also suffered a decline in population. In 1964, when Slains Estate was sold by auction, there were 47 beef, sheep and arable farms in the parish. In 2011 a mere handful of working farms remained.

The discovery of oil in the North Sea in the 1960s brought a new prosperity to the area. People have come from all over the world to work in the oil industry in and around Aberdeen and many of them have chosen to live in Collieston and Slains. However, despite the housing boom experienced by other small coastal villages, only a few modern houses have been built in Collieston with the result that the character of the village and the community spirit of the inhabitants have remained unchanged. Former fishermen's cottages, now modernised and well maintained, are still clustered on terraces overlooking the picturesque harbour and, in the parish of Slains, dilapidated farm buildings have been converted into stylish family homes.

Collieston from North

Cransdale, the bay immediately north of Collieston, was originally known as St Ternan's Haven, or Tarnshaven, after the saint who landed there in the fifth century having sailed from Banchory to Collieston to convert the Pictish inhabitants to Christianity. Centuries later the small inlet was regularly used by local smugglers for the landing of contraband. In the early nineteenth century a small fishing community was established at Cransdale. A salmon bothy, cooperage and fish house were built near the shore and the fishermen dried their nets on the nearby Hill of Cransdale. Fish was processed and packed into barrels which were then loaded onto carts and transported into Aberdeen by cadgers. Some years later the smaller boats were kept on the grassy slopes near the beach when the men were away to the herring fishing.

The Loch and Coast Guard Station, Collieston

Despite the dangers associated with smuggling, at the end of the 1700s a successful operative was run by two notorious men, Christie and Mitchell. At the time it was said that in Slains cottar houses you could get better brandy than could be found anywhere in the whole of Aberdeen. The situation was to change dramatically with the secondment of Malcolm Gillespie to the Collieston Preventive Station, subsequently the Coastguard Station seen here. From the day of his arrival in 1801, Gillespie worked fervently to bring about the demise of the local smuggling trade and by the time he left Collieston in 1807 he had destroyed numerous stills and seized thousands of gallons of spirits and numerous horses and carts. Nonetheless, Christie and Mitchell's operative continued until 1817 and few tears would have been shed in the Parish of Slains for 'the scourge of Collieston smugglers' when Malcolm Gillespie was publicly hanged in Aberdeen in 1827 after being found guilty of committing fraud and forgery.

Collieston Coastguard Station, formerly the Preventive Station, was built in the early 1800s on a cliff top south-west of the village. The isolated location would have been chosen so that the Preventive or Riding Officers could remain at a safe distance from the village yet have the ability to keep an eye on suspicious comings and goings at sea or on the links of Forvie. The Officer in Charge would have lived in the two-storey house with the lower ranks housed in the two-roomed terraced cottages, of which there were originally seven. In 1925 the full time Coastguard Company was disbanded leaving the volunteer Auxiliary Company to take on its duties of coastal watch and rescue. The lease for tenancy of the Coastguard Station officially expired on Whitsunday 1930 and the cottages were renamed Cluny Cottages, the Slains Estate having been owned since 1792 by the Gordon Family of Cluny Castle in Sauchen, Aberdeenshire. The new Collieston Coastguard Station was built in the late 1920s near the entrance to the village, in close proximity to the harbour.

HM Coastguard evolved from the Preventive Society, which was established in the eighteenth century to combat smuggling. The Scottish Coastguard was formed in 1819 and Life Saving Apparatus (L.S.A.) was installed in Collieston Coastguard Station in 1859. The Collieston L.S.A. was involved in many rescues throughout the nineteenth and twentieth centuries and regular training exercises were held along the Slains coast to ensure that rescue equipment was well maintained and personnel were kept up to date with all procedures. The rocket cart being hauled back to the station from the Forvie moors in this photograph from around 1930 was stored along with other rescue equipment in the rocket shed, a small building near the Coastguard Station. The rocket fired an attached line from the shore on to a stricken ship and enabled a breeches buoy to be brought into operation. At the end of the 1940s 'Rocket Practice' was moved from Cransdale, north of Collieston, to the cliff top above the Peerman Braes on Forvie moors where the Rocket Pole had been moved from its original position at the western end of the old Coastguard Station.

The Collieston LSA Company was awarded the Board of Trade Shield for best wreck service for 1931 for the gallant rescue of the ten-man crew of the Aberdeen trawler *Nairn* after the vessel had run aground during bad weather at Broadhaven, one mile south of Collieston, on 2 December that year. Within an hour of the alert at 10.30 p.m., the rescue was underway. Four rockets were fired from the top of the cliff but none held. The District Officer then ordered the rocket machine to be taken down to the rocks at the bottom of the cliffs. A fifth rocket was fired but the line parted. A sixth rocket was then fired but, as the crew hauled out the whip, it fouled the rocks and was cleared with great difficulty. The hawser was eventually hauled out and made fast around the wheelhouse. By 2.40 a.m. all of the crew had been brought safely ashore by breeches buoy. In addition to the company being awarded the Board of Trade Shield, Bronze Medals for Gallantry in Saving Life at Sea were also awarded to District Officer Smailes, Coastguardsman Shelley and Messrs Walker, Henderson and Robertson.

Another memorable day for the company, now renamed the Collieston CRC (Coast Rescue Company), was when the drifter *Stephens* ran aground on the Sands of Forvie in the early hours of 8 November 1956. The rescue was concluded at 4.40 a.m. when the last of the ten-man crew was brought safely ashore by breeches buoy. For this rescue the Collieston CRC was awarded the Shield for Best Wreck Service of the Year 1956. A presentation ceremony, seen here, was held in the old Village Hall. In 1966 the Collieston and Belhelvie companies were jointly awarded the Board of Trade Shield for the rescue of the crew of the *Semnos II* which ran aground on a sandbank near the mouth of the River Ythan near Newburgh. The presentation ceremony was held in the New Inn, Ellon. In the 1980s the Collieston CRC had a full complement of sixteen but in 1992 the company was regraded and reduced to a team of four. It had been suggested that the new teams would be called Fast Action Response Teams but the abbreviated form, FARTs, was thought to be rather inappropriate and they were instead called Initial Response Teams (IRTs).

In 1891 the Collieston Harbour Committee petitioned the Fishery Board to build a Harbour of Refuge at Collieston. Not only was a safe haven on the Aberdeen seaboard long overdue but a deeper harbour would also improve the prospects of the local fishing community. Permission was granted on 9 April 1894 and a survey of the harbour was carried out by Messrs D. & C. Stevenson of Edinburgh. Of the two entrances to Collieston's natural harbour, only one was to be retained. Many fishermen believed that the closing of the north entrance would allow sand from Aberdeen Bay to drift in and subsequently lead to problems of access for boats. Fishermen who wanted to block the south entrance were accused of putting personal convenience above common sense so that they could 'dander doon tae the yawls in their carpet slippers'. A vote resulted in a 50/50 split. After consulting with the engineer, Mr A.C. Melville, the committee chairman, the Rev. Greig, cast the deciding vote in favour of blocking the north entrance. The total cost of the project was £6,040. The Fishery Board donated £4,440 and the remaining £1,600 was raised by the fishing community. This photograph was taken while the work was being carried out.

An article in the *Banffshire Journal* of 21 October 1862 told of a memorable event held at Whiteness Hotel. The occasion was a dinner and dance to which the Collieston and Old Castle fishing communities were invited by Mr Gordon of Cluny, owner of Slains Estate, to celebrate his marriage in January of that year to Clara White at Bonchurch, Isle of Wight. The evening was brought to a close with the 300 guests dancing the Lang Reel of Collieston, by torchlight, on the flat ground beside the hotel, in honour of the recently married couple. Whiteness Hotel was also the focal point of celebrations after Lady Gordon Cathcart of Cluny Castle, Aberdeenshire, second wife of John Gordon of Cluny and owner of Slains Estate after her husband's death in 1878, laid the foundation stone of Collieston Pier on 17 October 1894. After the ceremony, a luncheon for 420 guests was held in a marquee in the grounds of the hotel while 250 local school children had tea in an adjoining marquee.

THE PIER, COLLIESTON D 1208

Ever since its construction in 1894/95 the pier, seen here in 1955, has had to withstand constant battering by the elements, especially during winter gales. During winter storms, winds from the east and north-east bring huge waves crashing over the pier wall, causing structural damage that has to be repaired during the spring and summer months. In December 1895 Mr Melville, civil engineer, wrote a letter to his on-site representative detailing recent damage done to the landward end of the pier. Another cause of damage, unforeseen by engineers of the project in the late nineteenth century, is that caused by motor vehicles trundling along the concrete surface.

Sir Douglas Ritchie and Richard 'Dick' Donald discuss the day's events at Collieston's first gala day in 1958. By the 1950s, after a number of years when no repairs had been carried out, the pier was in a dilapidated state. Sir Douglas, who had recently retired to his family home in the village, proposed the formation of a committee whose main aim would be to repair the damaged pier as well as the unique system of 'roadies' or paths that ran throughout the village. Collieston Amenities Committee was formed in 1957 and the first gala day was held the following year to raise money for this important on-going conservation work. The pier and 'roadies' were duly repaired and the gala day continues to be a popular annual event when money is raised for the upkeep of the pier and village.

Collieston's first gala day was held on Saturday, 19 July 1958. More than 1,000 visitors flocked to the village and £400 was raised to pay for urgent repairs to the pier. One of the highlights of the day was a tour of the hydrographical survey vessel HMS *Scott*, anchored in the bay and commanded by Captain Steve Ritchie, son of Sir Douglas. Frogmen from HMS *Scott* gave demonstrations to the crowd, a diver 'found buried treasure' containing coins and bags of goodies for the children, and the crowds lining the pier were entertained by members of Aberdeen's Dee Swimming Club's Crazy Gang. The day ended with a dance in the old Village Hall where not one, but two beauty queens were selected by Mrs R. Donald, Collieston, and Lieutenant Seubert. The title of 'Miss Collieston' went to Susan Jones with Helen Geddie the runner-up. The title of 'Mrs Collieston' went to Anne McBain with Norma Lewis the runner-up.

Yawls photographed in Collieston's natural harbour in the late nineteenth century, prior to the construction of the pier in 1894 when the village enjoyed a degree of prosperity as a fishing port. These boats had a crew of three or four men who would have had to row when there was no wind to assist them. The life of the long-line fisherman and his family was a hard one as each man was responsible for his own line of 600 hooks and at least 600 mussels had to be gathered by the women before each fishing trip. The line also needed to be regularly checked so that any damaged or lost hooks could be replaced. Fishermen went out in the early morning and returned in time for breakfast. After feeding the men, the women carried on with their work while the men rested before preparing the lines for the following day. According to the *New Statistical Account* of 1843, the local fishermen '. . . [catch] a great variety of fish . . . but what they chiefly depend upon are haddocks and cod which they catch in great abundance. They smoke and cure the haddocks principally for the Leith and Glasgow markets . . . .'

Women had an important part to play in helping the fishermen set off to the fishing grounds. In their 'shore shoon', i.e. with bare legs and skirts hitched up above their knees, they would wade into the cold water and lever the boat forward with their backs. After carrying out heavy stones for ballast, they would 'float' the men on to the boat by carrying them on their backs, piggy-back style, so that the fishermen's feet, in long leather boots saturated in sperm whale oil, would remain dry.

For a few years towards the end of the nineteenth century, the Collieston fishing fleet was of a considerable size. After each fishing trip the herring boats would be anchored in the safety of the recently constructed Harbour of Refuge. At the end of the fishing season it was customary to sail the herring boats up the River Ythan to a spot opposite Waterside Farm. When the tide was high enough the fishermen would borrow six or seven horses from the farm and, with the help of rollers, the boats would be dragged ashore to the piece of flat ground opposite the farm known as The Herring Boats.

Old Castle grew around the ruins of Old Slains Castle and became a popular haunt for smugglers in the eighteenth century. After the demise of the smuggling trade the inhabitants of Old Castle continued to make a good living from fishing. In the 1840s the village's fourteen houses had 48 inhabitants who were '. . . chiefly employed and wholly dependent upon white-fishing . . .' according to the *New Statistical Account*. At the beginning of the twentieth century the local fishing industry was in such decline that many young families had already left Old Castle. In March 1900 a terrible storm caused extensive damage to many of the houses perched on the exposed headland and the fishing boats were all destroyed, despite having been securely tied up on the rocky and grassy slopes some 30 feet above sea level. A collective decision was made by the remaining families to leave the village and move to Torry, Aberdeen, where it was hoped they could improve their living conditions and work prospects. Although most of the houses in Old Castle have long since disappeared, the few that remain have been modernised and are family homes.

A yawl sails into Collieston harbour in the early 1900s, by which time the local fishing industry was in severe decline. It is recorded that in 1880 there were 64 boats and 170 fishermen in Collieston but by 1900 the number of working boats had dropped dramatically to just sixteen. One of the reasons for the decline was the silting up of the harbour with sand coming in from Aberdeen Bay and the prohibitive cost of regular dredging that would have allowed the fishermen to use bigger boats. Another reason was the introduction of steam trawling. Many of the fishermen, particularly those with young families to support, had left Collieston around 1900 to join the steam trawlers working out of Torry or Peterhead where they could earn more money for less effort. Their wives were also keen to move when they realised that they could work as filleters for the fish merchants and get paid for their efforts, instead of having to work for their husbands for nothing.

Hawkley Bay, twelve feet long and built in Peterhead in 1926, is seen here being hauled over the sand to the safety of the Boatie Shore. By the late 1920s only fourteen boats continued to fish out of the village. There was a further decline in the 1930s when the number dropped to seven. However, the remaining fishermen were by this time quite elderly and were entitled to draw their weekly fisherman's pension so were not reliant on fishing as their only source of income. The boats may have been reasonably small but it nevertheless required strong arms to haul them up to the Boatie Shore. Despite the difficult task there were always willing bodies on hand after a fishing trip, usually other fishermen, but women and children were also called upon to help with the hard work if required.

Mussels, lugworm and mackerel were used as bait for the summer fishing and lugworm and sea anemones were used in winter. The best mussels came from the Ythan Estuary. The shells were prized open with sharp double-bladed knives and great concentration and stamina would have been required to avoid accidents. Although huge quantities of lugworm and mussels were used as bait, during the nineteenth century an attempt was made to ensure that stocks would be conserved and shared equally among the local fishing communities. As the *New Statistical Account* records: '. . . they [those baiting the fishing lines] are not allowed to go oftener than twice a-day, a regulation properly introduced by the tacksman of the river Ythan, to prevent the extravagant consumption of bait mussels, and in order to reserve a sufficient quantity for the neighbouring villages . . . .'

Wearing a traditional fisherman's gansey, James 'Jimicky' Walker baits lines. Most fishermen would have had at least two lines so that one would be in use while the other was being baited. Dried rushes were used as a base at the shallow end of a wicker or wooden scull. The baited line was paid into the deep end and its coils separated by more rushes laid crossways strip after strip so that when the line was shot over the side of the boat the hooks wouldn't foul one another. Once every year the lines had to be preserved in boiling cutch, taken from the bark of the South East Asian Betel Nut Tree. In Collieston this was done in March when the winter fishing was coming to an end. It was said that the barking of the lines gave them a better hold for hauling.

Andrew and Isabella Walker, 'Buckie and Bel', pictured shelling mussels and baiting lines. Expert hands could shell five mussels per minute but the actual baiting was a slow and laborious job as each line held approximately 600 hooks. In both winter and summer long lines were used for fishing and each line would have had several strings of baited hooks. A string had 60 hooks for a winter line and 100 hooks for a summer line. The hooks were held from lengths of hemp called snoods. These were tied to the backing by a clove hitch. A further two inches were plaited as a stiffener with a further twelve inches of single strand hemp before putting on a length of plaited horse hair, taken only from stallions or geldings, spun in two strands each with five hairs per strand. A haddock hook was then beat on with linen thread to make a total length on a small line, backing to hook, of between 36 and 40 inches.

John King, 'Johnny Dickie', pictured while 'reddin' and tippin'' the lines. 'Reddin'' was when the lines were tidied and untangled and any old bait was removed from the hooks. Damaged or lost hooks would also have to be replaced. 'Tippin'' referred to the tippins, the horsehair on which the hooks were fixed, when the horsehair would be wound round the hook shank and the hook placed backwards into the horsehair to prevent it from catching on the baiter's hand. Both tasks, although necessary, could often be both tedious and painful.

Left (upper and lower): After the catch was landed the fish would be carried over to the rocky foreshore and laid out ready for 'pairtin' when the fish would be sorted into those to be sold fresh, while the remainder would be preserved either by salting, smoking or drying. The job of cleaning and gutting was done by the women beside the stream that ran onto the beach near the Bog Wall (well). Using a sharp knife, each fish was split and cleaned thoroughly with a small scrubbing brush, made of heather stems bound together, to remove the blood from the bones and flesh. It was extremely important to make sure that not a drop of blood remained as even a mere trace meant that the fish would not keep.

Above: Collieston was famous for speldings, i.e. haddock or whiting, caught in the morning, split, cleaned, salted and dried by the sun and wind. At one time the fish were dried on rocks to the south of the village. The drying process was then moved to the Peerman Braes where the fish were hung on hooks attached to rails. Latterly the drying took place within the village. Fish were laid on a wooden board, tail in, to form a circle and sprinkled with salt. Layers of fish and salt were added until the pile was approximately one foot high. After a few days the fish were spread on wire netting racks and hung inside-out in dry weather and skin side uppermost when it rained. If eaten that same day speldings would be referred to as 'first day's fish' and roasted on a brick in front of the fire. Stored in a pillow case on top of the meal in the girnal (meal bin) during the winter month when fresh food was scarce, speldings would be cooked in a pan of boiling water to provide a simple, hot, nourishing meal.

Jean Ritchie pictured in the back garden of Sea View in 1902. The house was built by her brother, John Walker Ritchie (see pages 31 and 42). The women's work did not end with the cleaning and gutting of the fish; for some, the hardest work was still to come. With a creel full of 80 to 100 pounds of fresh or smoked fish on her back, the fishwife had to walk for miles to sell or barter her fish in the neighbouring towns and villages. Wearing a shawl to protect her shoulders, and a long skirt, hand-knitted jumper, hessian apron and stout shoes, the fishwife would set off early in the morning. Walking as far as Oldmeldrum, almost sixteen miles, she would call in at local farms along the way. The return journey to Collieston was no less arduous as, after selling her fish, she would then fill her creel with fresh farm produce such as butter, cheese, eggs, potatoes and oatmeal as well as other goods not stocked in the village shop.

This well-appointed granite building was built in 1886 as a bank and bank manager's house, but because of the decline in the local fishing industry it never functioned as such. It would appear to have lain empty for a few years until it became established as the village shop and post office in 1895. George (Geordie) Forrest, the first merchant/post master of Collieston, moved to the prestigious new premises from his original shop at the top of the Harbour Road at the place known locally as 'The Deal' (pronounced Dell). It was said that at Geordie's shop you could buy anything from a needle to an anchor. Postie Willie Watt in the pony and trap and Geordie Forrest, centre, are accompanied by Johnny Brand and his dog Princey. Johnny, a Crimean War veteran, came to Collieston to work as a diver when the pier was constructed in 1894. Collieston Post Office closed for business at the end of 2008 and the shop the following September after the retirement of the last owners, Abbie and Islay Stott.

The original church was built in 1599 and dedicated to St Ternan. Demolished and replaced by the present building in 1806, the only part of the original that remains is the walled and roofless Erroll's Aisle, the final resting place of several members of the Erroll family including Francis, ninth Earl of Erroll who died in 1631. In July of that year a solemn, torch-lit procession made its way from Slains Castle, Cruden Bay, to St Ternan's Chapel. Francis had expressed his desire to have a simple funeral and money that would have been spent on a lavish ceremony should instead be given to the poor. A major refurbishment of the church was undertaken in the early 1880s and the church was reopened in March 1882. According to the *Sentinel* of 15 March 1882, '. . . the audience was very large and attentive amounting to fully 500; and the church, being newly painted, had a very pleasant appearance . . . .' The site of the original manse, built in 1761, lay to the south-west of Slains Kirk in what is now the kirkyard. The new manse, designed by William Smith, was erected in its current location in 1876 and was sold in 1972 after the Rev. John Murray retired and Slains was united with Ellon Parish Church.

Slains Kirk was refurbished in the late 1920s. Most of the horseshoe gallery was demolished, boxes were removed and replaced with pews, and a pipe organ was installed. The Rev. John Ross, writing in the *Slains Church Supplement* of 1931, reported that, 'The demolition of the galleries showed that reconstruction was more necessary than anyone had suspected, for the joists supporting them were so decayed that it must have been a question of only a few years when they would have collapsed . . . .' The rededication service on Sunday, 31 August 1930, after which this photograph was taken, was led by the Very Rev. Principal Cairns DD, Moderator of the Presbytery of Aberdeen. Every pew was filled to capacity and extra chairs had to be brought in from nearby houses to provide additional seating. The pipe organ, built and installed by Mr Lawton of Pittodrie Organ Works, Aberdeen, was dedicated on 14 December the same year and played by the church organist, Mr Charles Arthur.

The Free Church mission and school was opened in July 1862. The house for the preacher and teacher was erected soon afterwards. Both church and house were built on the northern edge of the Sand Loch on land donated by John Gordon of Cluny. The £350 required to build the church was raised by contributions from friends of the Free Church and donations from Christians of other denominations. The balance was donated by the Church Building Committee of the Free Church. The interior of the building was divided by a partition in the middle so that it could function both as a church and a school. The upper part was fitted with pews and the lower part had moveable forms that could also double up as extra seating for the church. In 1919 church services were discontinued and the property was sold the following year. The church building was subsequently used as the village hall before it was sold to a local farmer and used as a combine harvester store. An article in the *Banffshire Journal* of 28 January 1862, long before the days of Health and Safety, described skating on the Sand Loch as 'excellent'.

Cars are parked on both sides of the road near the old Mission Hall, informally known as the 'Hallie', in this 1938 photograph. It is the building at the top of the road, just past the bend, with a car parked in front of its gable end. The walls of the one-roomed cottage were wood lined and covered with placards with passages from the scriptures. At one end of the room a raised platform served as a pulpit and forms for seating were arranged in rows. In the early 1900s the Sunday evening services were well attended and children would line up outside waiting for the door to open at 6.30 p.m. While they were singing hymns the adults would arrive, dressed in their Sunday best. The women wore jackets, long black skirts and black shawls on their heads and the men wore dark suits and shirts with hard collars and ties, or jerseys and peaked caps. Sheds, coated with Archangel tar, are dotted around the village. These are smokehouses where fish were hung on frames and smoked over wet sawdust and hardwood chips.

Pictured in the early 1900s, speldings hang on racks where the Adventure School once stood. This was immortalised in the poem 'Geordie Tough's Squeel', written in 1881 in the Buchan or Doric dialect, by former pupil John Walker Ritchie who attended in the 1860s when Geordie Tough was in charge: 'We'd neither Boord nor Squeel Inspectors, / An' nae new-fangl't Science Lect'rs / But, fit wis aften muckle better / He learnt us foo tae vreet a letter, / An' richtly train't oor han's an' min's / Tae readin' beuks an' reddin' lines, / Tae makin' sneeds an' keepin' coonts, / An' splicin' lines an' beetin' wints'. The poem goes on to relate that Geordie, despite being a strict disciplinarian, was well liked and respected by his charges who would watch for him going to school in the morning and race to see who would get to ring the bell. Each pupil had to take a book and a daily peat to school as payment in kind for receiving a rudimentary education.

Slains School and Schoolhouse in the early 1900s. The *Statistical Accounts of Scotland* for 1793 and 1843 both record the existence of a parish school in Slains when scholars had to pay to be taught Latin, Arithmetic, English and Writing. After the passing of the 1872 Education (Scotland) Act education became free and compulsory for all children between the ages of five and thirteen. In order to accommodate an increase in the number of children attending, the old parish school in Slains, built in 1835, was demolished. The new school, built to accommodate 100 pupils, was opened in January 1877 and an extension was added at the beginning of the twentieth century. Some 30 years after the opening of Slains School in 1877, the old schoolhouse was also demolished and rebuilt. For many years the schoolhouse, situated near the main Newburgh – Cruden Bay road, was home to the head teachers of Slains School. In the 1960s a new school was built to cater for the growing number of children living in the area. The old school was subsequently demolished in 1968 and the space that it occupied became the school playground.

The teacher and pupils of Collieston School in 1913. This was opened in 1877 and, having passed the government examination on completion of her training at the Church of Scotland Training College in Aberdeen, Miss Mary Ganson was appointed the school's first head teacher by the School Board of Slains. From June 1894, when there were 80 children on the school roll, to October 1899, the head teacher was Mrs Isabella Kemp, whose entry in the Collieston School Log for Friday, 19 October 1894 states: '. . . Very good attendance this week. A holiday being given out on Wednesday, it being day of laying of the foundation stone of New Harbour by Lady Gordon-Cathcart. Other work as usual . . . .' The school roll dropped dramatically after the demise of the local fishing industry and closed in 1922 with the result that children had to walk to Slains School. By 1932 the school roll had increased sufficiently for the school to reopen but this proved to be a short-term reprieve and Collieston School closed permanently on 1 July 1949. The last head teacher was Miss Gladys Robertson.

In the 1920s the Muckle Reid (Road) had become difficult to negotiate safely so the local council appointed a Special Sub-committee to carry out an inspection. In 1924 the Surveyor reported that it was impracticable to straighten or improve the bend but, as a suitable alternative, a new road could be built into the village from west of Kirkton Farm, passing Slains Manse and Glebe and emerging near the village post office and shop (Slains Manse is on the left of this photograph and the Glebe behind it). In January 1925 a plan was submitted with an estimated cost of £670. The committee unanimously approved the plan and estimate, subject to the adjustment of claims for compensation by the landlord and tenant of the ground. It was remitted to the Road (Emergency) Sub-Committee to settle the claim and to apply to the Ministry of Transport for a grant towards the cost. Later that year a grant of £247 was awarded but, by that time, the cost of the project had increased to £988 with the result that the committee unanimously decided not to proceed with the new road.

LOW TOWN, COLLIESTON.

North of the pier is Cransdale where a round hill of solid rock contains a fissure called the Needle's E'e, through which the sea pounds violently during an easterly gale. North of Cransdale is St Catherine's Dub named after a Spanish warship, *Santa Catarina*, which sank off the rocky headland during the late sixteenth century while trying to land arms in support of the Earl of Erroll's Catholic uprising of 1594 against King James VI. In 1855 the minister of Slains Kirk, the Rev. James Rust, succeeded in raising one of the guns from the warship. According to the Rev. J.B. Pratt in his book *Buchan*, '. . . Mr Rust had this gun mounted on a carriage, and for long it stood at the manse of Slains; it is now at Haddo House . . . a diving party employed by the Countess of Erroll, in 1876, raised two and an anchor, which were sent by the Countess to Her Majesty at Balmoral; and the largest and most complete cannon in every respect was got on 25th August 1880, and is now in possession of a London firm . . . .'

The ruins of Old Slains Castle lie on a rocky headland a few miles north of Collieston. The castle had been the stronghold of the Hays of Erroll since the fourteenth century when King Robert the Bruce gave the land of Slains in Buchan to Sir Gilbert Hay, fifth Baron of Erroll, in recognition of his loyal service during the Wars of Independence. In 1594 the castle was almost completely destroyed by gunpowder and cannon, under the personal supervision of King James VI after Francis Hay, ninth Earl of Erroll, made the decision to side with the Earl of Huntly in rebelling against the King. Francis was forced to flee into exile but his wife did not to go with him, choosing instead to move into nearby Clochtow Farmhouse where she remained for a number of years and referred to herself as the 'Guidwife of Clochtow'. Francis returned from exile in 1597 and had his lands restored but, instead of rebuilding the ruined Slains Castle, he chose to build a new one at Cruden Bay.

In the 1950s Slains had a thriving and successful football club. Football practice was on Monday evenings when the manager, Andy Simpson, would announce his team selection for the next game. As well as playing against teams such as Foveran, Cruden and Ardallie in the Buchan Amateur League, Slains also played friendly matches, travelling to places such as St Fergus or Rosehearty. League games were played in the evenings, usually mid week, from April to late July. Slains played their home games at The Feu and the Cup Final was always held at The Halfway House, on the road to Mintlaw. Supporters had plenty to cheer about in 1951 and 1956, the years when Slains Football Team won the Buchan Amateur League Cup. The team was disbanded in the 1960s.

COLLIESTON

Pictured in the early years of the twentieth century, several abandoned and dilapidated cottages bear testimony to the exodus of many young fishermen and their families from Collieston to Torry and Peterhead. However the fact that fishing still played an important part in village life, albeit on a small scale, is evident in the number of black smokehouses scattered throughout the Low Town area. Cows graze on the grassy slopes of the Bog where natural spring water runs from the Bog Wall (well). Every morning before going off to school the 'herdie' had to lead the cows to the grassy slopes in the Bog or up to the Rivie, the grassy promontory dividing The Cliff from Cransdale. At the end of the school day, the young boy would then have to shoo the cows back up the brae to be milked at the byre at the dairy in High Town. In the centre of the photograph, the three terraced cottages in the Bog were built in 1887, the year of Queen Victoria's Golden Jubilee, and the row was originally called Jubilee Terrace. The row of ruined cottages on the lower right is where the beach shelter and toilet block now stand.

Andrew Walker, baker, was proprietor of the Bakery and Refreshment Rooms until the early 1920s. The building, a single-storey rubble and harled cottage with a turf roof and wooden extensions, has a very high chimney that would have created extra updraught for the bakery oven. Sometime during the 1920s an old First World War Nissen hut was brought over from Lenabo Airfield, west of Peterhead, and used as a tearoom which was run by Andrew's daughter Christina until the late 1930s. After the Nissen hut, a wooden shed was used as the tearoom. During the 1920s and '30s Spelding Teas at The Refreshment Rooms were very popular with visitors to Collieston. A Spelding Tea consisted of oatcakes and butter, two grilled speldings, tea and cakes, and could be purchased for the sum of one shilling and sixpence (7.5 pence). Although significantly extended and now a family home, the property is still known as The Bakery.

Low tide reveals the channel through the rocky foreshore where the boats were hauled up to the safety of the Boatie Shore. After removing the fleshy parts of mussels for baiting the lines, the empty shells were scattered over the narrow paths that criss-crossed the village, the rights of way called roadies. One of the main roadies, the Shellie Brae, winds its way up the steep side of the Ness from the Boatie Shore in Low Town to the Braehead in High Town. It is still very much in use today, especially for people who live in High Town and like to bring home containers of natural spring water from the Bog Wall (well).

Pictured in the early twentieth century the fishwives appear to be gutting fish on the pier while watched by a well-dressed lady, but this would have been set up purely for the photograph as fish were always cleaned and gutted on rocks near the Bog Wall (well) and never on the pier. It does, however, give an insight into dress styles of the period, for both men and women. The house at the end of the pier, 15 The Cliff (the house with the small window in its gable end seen in the centre of the photograph), was where Aircraftsman T.E. Shaw (Lawrence of Arabia) and two companions stayed for a short time in 1930. In a letter to his publisher F.N. Doubleday, Lawrence wrote that the house had been lent to him by the owner Mrs Ross and he described the cottage as '... the nearest hovel to the high-tide mark ....' The men did not do much cooking and Lawrence told his publisher how they were fed three times a day by 'Mrs Baker-and-butcher' in her parlour at the bakery. When he wasn't taking his turn at sweeping floors, fetching water and coal and drying swimsuits, Lawrence liked to spend time sitting by the fire thinking while eating pandrops – peppermint sweets unknown to him prior to his stay in Collieston.

Speldings are drying on racks outside this house built of divots and sods. Long since gone, it was once home to Jinsy's Meggie, the local howdie (midwife). Sea View, the house in the background, overlooks the harbour and was built in the early 1880s by John Walker Ritchie for his parents, George and Janet Ritchie (see pages 25 and 31). John, author of the poem 'Geordie Tough's Squeel', left Collieston to seek his fortune. Although he settled in Manchester where he married a local girl and became a successful businessman, John never lost his love of Collieston and brought his family regularly to spend holidays at Sea View. Sadly, in the summer of 1890, John (36), his father George (62) and local boy Alexander Stott (15) drowned in a tragic boating accident. According to local witnesses, the boat had been sailing along about half a mile off Collieston and heading for shore when it suddenly disappeared. The fishermen quickly manned their boats and set off to the spot where the craft had gone down, but they found no sign of survivors or wreckage. John's body was discovered a few days later and buried in Slains Kirkyard but the bodies of George and Alexander were never found.

The manse garden at Slains Kirk provided food for the minister until the land was required for an extension to the kirkyard, consecrated after the Armistice service on Sunday, 9 November 1930, by the Rev. James Ross. The watch-house in the north-east corner was built as a shelter for grieving relatives as they kept watch over a loved one's grave in the days when bodysnatching was rife. A gravestone near the entrance to the kirk bears the inscription: 'In memory of Philip Kennedy who lived sometime in Ward of Slains who died the 19th Decr. 1798 Aged 38 years.' A farm worker, Philip was one of a group of smugglers involved in the landing of Holland gin at Cransdale. Unaware that they had been betrayed, the smugglers were ambushed by revenue officers and Philip was fatally wounded during the violent skirmish. He managed to crawl to Kirkton Farm, near Slains Kirk, where he died, stretched out on a deiss (bench) in the farmhouse kitchen. His last words were, 'If a' had been as true as me, the prize wid a' been safe and I widna a' been bleeding to death.' Kirkton Farm was a sizeable arable and beef farm. In addition to the substantial four-bedroomed farmhouse, there was a bothy, covered cattle court, two cow byres, root house, hay barn, threshing barn with food store and loft, and two chicken houses.

At Smiddyhill Farm in 1919, when this photograph was taken, sheep were clipped by hand. Although electric clippers arrived on Aberdeenshire farms just before the outbreak of the Second World War, it was not until the 1950s that they were widely used in Slains. Farmers clipped their own sheep until the early 1970s when they began to employ professional sheep shearers to do the work instead. Farmers had their sheep marked with a special paint that could be washed out of the fleece after clipping and the same distinguishing marks were kept by families for generations. Sheep were dipped to help control fly related problems. Prior to 1910, the farmer at Forvie used a wooden dipper which was subsequently moved from Forvie to Smiddyhill where it was set in concrete in 1916. For the following ten to fifteen years the dipper at Smiddyhill was used by several of the neighbouring farms and at dipping time children would often have to walk over the fields to get to Slains School because the roads were crowded with sheep.

In 1782 the harvest was very late and the crop yield was poor because of the unseasonal cold, wet weather. Despite the so-called 'snowy hairst', the state of the parish of Slains was recorded as being in a much better shape than other parishes in Aberdeenshire. During the early years of the 1800s a large extent of waste land was drained and cultivated but, apart from the sandy links at Forvie and the raised peat bog of Lochlundie Moss, there was very little land in the parish that was unsuitable for cultivation or grazing. Tenant farmers in Slains were rightly described in the *New Statistical Account* as: '. . . most industrious and enterprising and readily adopt any new improvement, either in the breed of cattle or mode of farming . . . .' Although the steam plough had been introduced into Aberdeenshire at Brownhill Farm in April 1872 by Mr John Gordon, owner of Slains Estate, horses continued to be used on most farms until the mid-twentieth century when the impact of two world wars, mechanisation and the arrival of electricity in the 1950s revolutionised farming in the Parish of Slains.

Draught horses and farm workers pictured at Smiddyhill in the early 1900s when unmarried male farm servants lived either in a bothy, a small one or two roomed building, or a chaumer, a room in the farm steading. Conditions in both were very basic. The men had to sleep on 'chaff' (straw) mattresses in wooden box beds, and clothes were hung on pegs on the wall and any valuables were locked in a 'kist' (chest). There was no fire in the chaumer but the men only went there to sleep as they had their meals in the farmhouse kitchen where they had the customary right to sit by the fire until 9 p.m. When sold by auction on 16 July 1964 at the Station Hotel, Aberdeen, there were 47 beef, sheep and arable farms on the Slains Estate. Smiddyhill Farm was described as an arable farm of approximately 132 acres. The stone-built farmhouse was included in the sale as were the farm buildings which consisted of a deep litter house, bothy, tractor shed and cow house, fuel store, loose box, barn, granary loft, three implement sheds (one with loft), cattle yard, calf house, cow byre, and two stables with lofts.

The Marine Hotel can be seen in the upper left of this photograph behind The Bakery (painted white). Its guests enjoyed hot and cold running water and inside bathrooms, a stark contrast to the basic sanitation in the village where conditions were much the same as they had been in 1832 when Asiatic Cholera was brought to the village from Leith in a fisherman's boat. In the space of six weeks 23 of Collieston's 350 inhabitants died. Sanitation in Collieston was discussed at a Slains Parochial Board Meeting in 1873 because stagnant water and 'more offensive matter' had begun to collect between the houses and build up against the walls. The meeting found that '. . . there is an entire absence of privies, a fact which is in many places offensively evident . . . .' In the early 1900s refuse depots (middens) were constructed in both High Town and Low Town where villagers could dispose of household waste. In 1922 lavatory accommodation was provided, for women only, at a cost of £25 9s 3d. A few years later other facilities were provided and, although referred to as public latrines, they were only available to households for an annual charge of 5s per key. By 1928, 22 houses in Collieston had their own WC but 34 houses were still without running water.

The Cliff, with number 15 on the extreme left. For many centuries villagers had to fetch water from one of the natural springs such as the Bog Wall (well) in Low Town. In 1900 a modern drainage system was installed to bring a supply of water from nearby natural springs to the extended and refurbished Marine Hotel. Water was subsequently pumped by means of hydraulic rams from the reservoir at Perthudden into several stand pipes in the village. Further improvements were undertaken in the 1920s when the Preventive Station's disused boat house was bought by the local authority and converted into a pumping station, thus paving the way for every home in the Collieston to have its own supply of running water. After the demise of the local fishing industry the increase in the number of holidaymakers coming to Collieston was a great boost to the local economy. However, the shortage of water became such a problem that at one time in the 1920s a stop-cock had to be fixed to the main pipe so that the water supply to Low Town could be shut off periodically to allow an adequate supply of water to houses in High Town.

Pictured around 1910, Margaret Ingram does the family wash in a wooden tub outside her home in Low Town. While it was advisable to drink only fresh spring water, it was customary to use rain water for general household purposes and most families would have had a barrel for collecting rain water for washing hair, pots and clothes. No mod cons were available to lighten the housewife's load and, with large families the norm, washing clothes was always labour intensive. A lull between fishing seasons meant a welcome break from lugging creels of fish round the countryside, but it brought about another kind of drudgery for the women – the annual blanket-washing. Blankets were sometimes laid out in front of the house, but it was customary for a cart to come round the village collecting pots, washing tubs and blankets and transport them to the Sand Loch where fires would be lit, water in the pots would be boiled, and blankets would be washed and spread out to dry.

Below: A view taken from the Rivie, the promontory between Collieston and the bay at Cransdale.

COLLIESTON FROM EAST

In 1862 Collieston was reported in the *Banffshire Journal* as '. . . very much frequented by pic-nic parties . . . ' and as '. . . a place of fashionable resort by residents in the surrounding country, who come and improve their health by sea-bathing and change of air . . . .' Since the late-nineteenth century Collieston has been a popular destination for school outings and the pupils at the Bruce-Hay Girls' School in Slains, founded in 1868 by Mrs Hay of Collieston in memory of her husband and two brothers, enjoyed an annual outing to Collieston and the Links of Forvie until the school closed in 1906. One such outing took place in August 1880 when Miss Allan and her pupils assembled at the school and were transported in six horse-drawn carts as far as Slains Manse where they were met by the Rev. and Mrs Greig. Marching in pairs the children sang as they made their way through the village, stopping for tea and cake at the home of Mrs Hay. The school party continued on their way until they reached the links of Forvie where they played games and ran races.

From the 1920s to the late 1940s George Ross, in partnership with his cousin Alexander Cruickshank, ran the Newburgh Bus Service and Collieston was also included in this much-needed transport link. After making his family home in Collieston, George would motorcycle to Newburgh to collect the bus then drive to Collieston to begin the daily journey to Aberdeen. In the evening, after all the passengers had been safely delivered home, George would take the bus back to the garage in Newburgh and then motorcycle back to his home. Latterly, the bus was kept overnight in a garage near the village shop and post office. The bus service was well used by many local people at a time when few people had cars as it enabled them to either study or work in Aberdeen and return to their homes in Collieston at the end of the day.

THE HARBOUR, COLLISTON. CLTN. 8.

In the 1940s and '50s demand for holiday lets in Collieston was such that it was not uncommon for house owners to move to an outside shed or upstairs to the attic so that rooms could be rented out. At the beginning of the twentieth century when few people had cars, transport was available for hire from the New Inn, Ellon, and a horse and carriage would travel to and from Collieston every Wednesday and Saturday during the summer months. Some years later the Newburgh Bus Service provided a useful link between Collieston and those members of the fishing community who had moved to live and work in Torry in the early 1900s, many of whom still owned houses in the village. At the start of the summer holidays George Ross would drive over to Torry, load furniture onto the roof rack of his bus and bring the families and their belongings back to their beloved Collieston, a welcome contrast to the hustle and bustle of city life. Families with young children would spend as much of the summer as possible in their seaside cottages.